Open Government Data and Implications for mobileGovernment

Towards a More Transparent and Efficient Governance

Emre Simsek and Ibrahim Kushchu

mobileGov UK Series on mGovernment: Vol IV

December 2016

ISBN: 191203770X
ISBN-13: 978-1912037704

DEDICATION

To all those who believe in the power of sharing knowledge ...

mobileGov UK's Series on MobileGovernment:

Over the years mobileGov UK has accumulated significant resources in the form of articles, reports, training materials and presentations, mostly gathered from actual projects completed. The aim of these series is to share this accumulated knowledge via series of volumes, each of which contains essential information on eGovernment, transforming the public sector organizations and mobileGovernment.

Please also see other volumes in this collection: 'mobileGov UK's Series on mGovernment' to access a spread of knowledge on research and practice of mobileGovernment.

This Particular Volume in Your Hand is about open government data and its implications for mobileGovernment.

CONTRIBUTIONS

The field of mobileGovernment as a practice has been growing significantly and implemented successfully by various governments since mobileGov's early efforts from 2000s by valuable contributions of students in Japan, the researchers, colleagues and many professionals from all around the world, all of whom, deserve gratitude and appreciation. Thanks to all wholeheartedly.

The team at the mobileGov UK and its project partners are important contributors to this collection on mobileGovernment. Without their encouragement, hard work and efforts none of these volumes would be produced.

The contributing authors to this specific volume are **Emre Simsek** and **Ibrahim Kushchu** of mobileGov UK. It starts with providing and account of what is understood by open data in the public sector and through analysis and implications, it ends discussing opportunities and challenges for mobileGovernment.

.

CONTENTS

Abstract

This is the age of data revolution. Governments, businesses, and individuals increasingly rely on accurate and timely data in their decision making. New technologies are taking place to increase the amount, quality, speed and usability of data; new tools are being developed for dissemination of data; and new methods are being invented to derive valuable information from raw data.

There are however new challenges with respect to how data should be collected, how it should be stored, managed, transferred and ultimately how to make the most out of this ever growing, so called "big data". Governments seek to have tools to collect and meaningfully analyze the data to support their policy decisions; businesses strive to know the facts for their business investments and individuals want to access relevant data anywhere and anytime they need to make decisions. Moreover, developers are extensively using the "big" and "open" public data to create new applications for government agencies, businesses and individuals.

Throughout this paper, we will discuss what makes the public data really "open"; why is it crucial for government transparency, citizen engagement and service innovation; what are the steps governments should take to publish their data; and moreover how data openness contributes to mobileGovernment implementations. Among all the other potential outcomes, we highlight Open Government Data's economical and social benefits by unleashing the power of ever growing amount of "big data" in favor of more efficient governments and empowered citizens and businesses.

It is highly critical that all the stakeholders realize the benefits and opportunities that OGD brings to the table, and work in collaboration for data openness as well as its efficient use for better public services and innovative service applications for governments, businesses and citizens. Although the discussions about the relevance of data openness in public sector are significantly encouraging, there has not been a single country yet to realize the full potential of government data openness due to certain setbacks. Therefore we will showcase the good practices and steps required to open public data to serve as a guideline to governments.

***Keywords:** open government data, mobileGovernment, innovative public services, efficient government, big data*

Emre Simsek and Ibrahim Kushchu

1. Introduction

Huge amount of data that governments are holding represents a special topic of interest because utilizing the data in an open and efficient manner has several positive implications for each and every government departments as well as for businesses and citizens: Better policies, greater transparency and accountability of government agencies, sounder investments, more accurate decisions, greater citizen engagement etc.

Open Government Data (OGD) has been one of the hottest discussion points in governance since early 2000s among public activists and leading governments globally. The basic idea behind OGD is that the data held by public sector should be a resource that is open to public for commercial and non-commercial purposes. Public sector holds bulks of institutional data as well as personal and statistical data. OGD activists point out that this public data has a value to the government agencies but the unrealized potential value of OGD is that citizens, other public sector institutions and entrepreneurs may also have huge benefits through OGD initiatives. Therefore, the potential of OGD should be unleashed at first by strong political commitment.

Opening government data and making it a public resource, however, is a daunting task and should be taken into action with a strategic proactive approach involving a strong backing from government authorities as well as a "pull" demand from citizens and businesses.

Although there are variety of resources available on open government data, in this paper we will present this topic with its implications for mobileGovernment.

Structure of this paper is as follows. We will start with a brief history of OGD in the following section and how OGD gained momentum since late 2000s. We will then investigate the benefits of opening government data for government institutions, as well as businesses, citizens and other stakeholders. Following that, we will lay out the general principles of open data, and under which circumstances the public data may be considered as really "open". Then, we will put forward a step by step guideline to open government data. Lastly, we will continue with what open data brings to the table in the case of mobileGovernment with an analysis of opportunities and challenges and conclude.

1.1. Brief History of Open Government Data

Back in 2006, a variety of governments started taking a proactive initiative in which they had begun releasing datasets among public websites. Since 2009, the OGD initiative has taken a leap forward with the two large milestones; first, launching of data.gov for the United States of America in May 2009, and second, along with the launching of data.gov.uk for the United Kingdom in January 2010. These initiatives fuelled the discussion of a pressing requirements for opening government data.

Consequently, international institutions such as World Bank and OECD have been calling for data openness and urging governments to start making their information available to the public in a machine-readable and reusable format without discrimination. In 2013, following the signing of Open Data Charter in which G8 countries pledged to make all public sector data available to the public, the global movement for data openness in public sector has begun to gain prominence. In 2014, the UN and the G20 countries followed the suit by announcing that a "Data Revolution" was needed for the global development goals to be reached.

2. Outcomes of Data Openness in Public Sector

All governments have huge amounts of public data collected on an annual basis. Also, great deal of them are structured data that can be used and reused by other interested parties. The information and data which are being generated continuously ranging from anything between statistical economic data sets, all the way to health care, public safety, traffic and spatial information. These are great resources that no country have used up to their full potential yet, with regards to government transparency and efficiency. Moreover, external economic benefits of opening public data are yet to be fully discovered and its innovation potential yet to be unleashed. It is widely accepted that data openness in public sector has beneficial implications for government transparency, government efficiency, and service innovation. Governments and their agencies might expect the following outcomes with their initiatives of opening government data:

- **Citizen engagement:** OGD opens up engagement paths to citizens in analyzing government actions, getting involved in public decisions and support government services with mechanisms of feedbacks, complaints and voting. Enhanced transparency of government actions will increase government departments' accountability, and an increase in communication between citizens and the government would represent an increased trust in government services.

- **Policy Analysis:** Releasing government data publicly will allow revealing facts of public importance and analyzing the interrelations of public policy and its outcomes. Policy makers and researchers would need concrete data to analyze in order to make relevant policy regulations and necessary investments (i.e. Crime rates, accident frequency, tourism investment etc.).

- **Governments' internal efficiency and cooperation:** As the public data becomes more available and accessible, government departments' interaction and cooperation will increase to raise overall government efficiency and service quality. Service delivery time gains, cost effective data management, business reprocessing, an increase in the interoperability between a variety of systems in place, and reduction in government employees responding to public record requests, are just few areas that OGD will have direct positive impact in public sector.

- **Service Innovation:** Opening up public data for commercial and noncommercial use will lead to all sorts of new informational and interactive services by public and private sector. New and upcoming businesses will take advantage of the available information in order to produce a variety of new products and bring in new services they can offer by utilizing the released datasets.

2.1. Implications for MobileGovernment

OGD initiatives have several positive implications on mobileGovernment development that governments are discovering rather slowly. Making use of government datasets in mobile platforms leads to infinite possibilities in mobile application and service innovation. Published datasets are huge resources that can be utilized effectively on mobile channel as several leading examples around the globe proved so such as Singapore, United States, Hong Kong etc. Government departments as well as private initiatives from businesses and citizens spread the creativity to a wider ecosystem and results in services and applications designed by the contribution of the end-users and field experts.

Making public data available and reusable without any sort of restriction, thus, is another key enabler for mobileGovernment development as it already is for eGovernment. Opportunities for mobileGovernment stemming from OGD initiatives are discussed in a broader sense in the fifth section.

3. Principles of OGD

In December 2007, a meeting was held by 30 government advocates in California, US. The idea was to develop the concept of open government, define the principles of open government data and emphasize how crucial data openness is for democracy and transparency. After that meeting the following 8 principles of Open Government Data was announced, and they are widely accepted as prerequisites of OGD:

Principles of Open Government Data

Government data is made public with the following principles:

1. Complete: All public data can be available without limitations in terms of privacy security or privileges.

2. Primary: Open data is as it is at the source with no modifications or alterations.

3. Timely: it is made available quickly to be useful and valuable.

4. <u>Accessible</u>: it is available to all ranges of users for various purposes.

5. Machine processable: it is structured and can be read and processed by machines.

6. Non-discriminatory: it is open to anyone unconditionally.

7. Non-proprietary: it does not have restrictive formats or ownerships.

8. License-free: it does not come with IP rights or trade secrets, though certain privacy, privileges or security restrictions may apply.

Source: <u>https://public.resource.org/8_principles.html</u>

As seen above, in order for data to be categorized as open data, it must be available to all those who wish to use it and data must provide as much detail as possible in a timely manner.

Furthermore, the data must be available to public with the ease of accessibility, and there should be no constraint to reuse the data or combine it with other datasets to create meaningful analysis or a new service.

These principles have straightforward implications about the how governments should publish their data.

1. Reaching out to published data should be easy for all involved - data should be well classified, searchable, properly formatted and in convenient forms. Datasets should be backed with metadata that describes and tags what data is about. Openly shared data catalogs may prove helpful to parties that look for certain kind of data among the huge datasets that public sector holds.

2. Released data should be suitable for commercial and noncommercial reuse since this ability is the key element that permits development and advancement of innovative products and services to take place. Datasets should be in a form that allows people to derive certain data out of it and combine it with other relevant data from other sources that may lead to a new understanding, an innovative service or a product. Machine readability is the fundamental prerequisite for this. For instance, XML and CSV are widely used machine readable and configurable formats and they are applicable for many types of datasets. Datasets should be well instructed as to the methods of data collection and the source of the presented data.

3. Datasets should be accessible by being released in open formats meaning that access to data should not be restricted by a license to use certain software, if possible. Commonly used formats should be chosen wherever possible in order to enhance the usability of the data by the largest possible segments.

4. Datasets should be accessible in bulk rather than in segments and continuously updated. There is always a possibility for special software to pull query based data from bulk datasets, therefore programmers may create new applications and services by utilizing these datasets. Efforts should be undertaken to link the existing data so that the datasets are combined together in reference to each other. In this way, finding relevant and related data will be easier for those who needs and require them.

Publishing government data solely is not enough for promoting innovation. Therefore, restrictions on the reuse of data should be abolished to the extent that no legal rights and privacy concerns are breached. In other words, any person or entity should be able to access the data without any justification or authorization.

3.1. Implications for MobileGovernment

Same principles apply for utilization of OGD in mobileGovernment projects. Moreover some of these principles are reinforced with the inclusion of mobileGovernment in the equation. For instance, accessibility principle for OGD is taken a step further with mobile platforms utilizing the released datasets. The principle that the data should be non-discriminatory also is broadened by the inclusion of mobile users to access government data services on mobile devices (i.e. real time traffic information).

4. Guidelines to Open Government Data

The procedure to open government data to public access depends on various country specific circumstances such as: the available infrastructure, political dedication, public demand, budget restrictions, institutional acceptance, employee and citizen capacity and so on. Governments, therefore, should start from setting achievable targets for OGD in the country context and then plan for the rollout of the entire project.

In this section, we are going to lay out the *fundamental steps* to open government data that applies in general context. There will inevitably be other relevant steps to be taken for every different country, however, the following guideline should display the generic idea for the governments to follow.

Step 1. Define Your Goals

Every government faces unique challenges and has different opportunities in Open Government Data, as is the case with every other development. Therefore, analyzing the unique requirements for

OGD and setting up achievable and suitable targets is the first step in OGD initiatives. It is important that goals for open data are clearly stated with reference to the overall digital strategy and expected outcomes. Defining targets earlier will allow projection of potential outcomes of OGD, therefore making it easier to gather other stakeholders around a strategy. Policy decisions should be based on the initial goals and milestones should be set for opening up public data for every government department that are involved and also about when to expect the desired outcomes for each and every public body as well as for the whole of government.

Set of Actions

Action I.   Analyze country specific circumstances regarding public data with reference to barriers and opportunities.

Action II.   Set short-term, medium-term and long-term targets for OGD.

Action III.   Clearly document the overall Open Government strategy.

Action IV.   Communicate the expected outcomes and benefits of OGD in all levels of government as well as other stakeholders.

Action V.   Bring the stakeholders around the same OGD strategy and base policy decisions for the benefit of all stakeholders involved.

Step 2. Design the Rollout Plan in Accordance with Current Priorities

As discussed, OGD brings in several benefits to governments, businesses and citizens. Some countries pursue transparency and accountability as the main target of OGD, whereas others focus more on the economic benefits, efficiency gains and new service creation through OGD. It should be clearly identified which of these goals are the most urgent in specific country case and only then a rollout plan should be deployed.

By clearly identifying the urgent priorities of the country and showcasing the progression that open data has to offer for these priorities, policy makers will be able to get stakeholders together and quickly gain the momentum necessary for successfully having a long lasting open data scheme. Priorities could be: increasing government efficiency, investing on government transparency, improving public safety, improving health services etc.

Set of Actions

Action I.   Analyze what your government's most urgent requirements are that are related to OGD.

Action II.   Study and document what OGD may offer for these requirements.

Action III. Set out a rollout plan with milestones taking your priorities into account.

Action IV.   Clearly announce the reasoning of the set priorities as well as the rollout plan itself publicly.

Step 3. Prioritize the Data to be Released

Prioritization of the data to be released depends on several factors such as: the goal of the overall project, costs involved, public demand, existing methods of data handling, existing laws and regulations etc. It is important to prioritise in line with the goals and pursued outcomes of the whole project and start prioritising from there. Therefore, investigating which datasets would contribute most to those goals is vital.

It is generally a good idea to start on a smaller scale by simply focusing on a few carefully chosen datasets. Usability of the data is crucial and rather than publishing big amounts of public data in low quality formats, it is better to publish the more usable datasets first and then focus on improving the other data for better usability. Out of these datasets, those that require the least effort may be published rather quickly.

Understanding public demand is a key component of prioritising open data policies. Tracking the web traffic of government websites which offer certain data as well as considering how many requests there are for public records, and look into what data would be able to fulfill the satisfaction of the public may give robust opinion about the demand for data.

For engaging public opinion in open data policies, it is critical to find ways to communicate with the public and find out what kind of data they would be interested in having access to and what they would find most useful. Public surveys, online polls, feedback mechanisms, public discussions and idea competitions may prove to obtain better insight of public demand for open data. Researchers and businesses should also be mobilized to engage in policy decisions regarding OGD.

Legal alignment is also a factor determining the priorities for OGD: Publishing government data should address both security and privacy concerns as well as be aligned with the legal base, laws and regulations.

Cost projections may be another aspect of prioritisation since many times opening up government data comes with a cost and staff time. While it may be said that the wiser thing is to start from low cost projects, it should be noted that sometimes projects with significant costs might be of priority due to their return on investment or enabling nature for other benefits. In these cases cost factor should not be limiting the goals of the overall strategy.

Set of Actions

Action I.   Take initial and urgent goals of OGD as reference and investigate which data are most vital for your goals.

Action II.   Start publishing from better quality data that requires the least effort and cost.

Action III.   Analyze public demand for data by taking past requests for public data.

Action IV.   Gather public opinion through surveys, feedbacks, polls and other forms of engagement mechanisms.

Action V.   Consider the data to be opened in relation to the existing legal structure and regulations.

Action VI.   Consider the cost factors of opening public data.

Step 4. Protect Private and Sensitive Data

When it comes to legislations and directives which already exist and are in reference to the accessibility to public information, an open data policy is a necessity. Bulks of data released by governments may hold individual data of people that are private and sensitive, or private information about businesses that are not to be disclosed. Therefore, the legal policy should be aligned to combine with public access law exemptions with respect to to sensitive information for reasons such as privacy or security.

Also, there may be a need for new legislations and institutional regulations to enable the full potential of open government data. Digital laws should be inspected in order to comply with the technological advancements and institutional directives should be adjusted to involve open data principles so as to lift the legal barriers in OGD.

Set of Actions

Action I.   Analyze sensitive datasets that may disclose private and confidential data.

Action II.   Restrict certain datasets while publishing government data and make a listing of the restricted data.

Action III.   Analyze what legal adjustments should be made to lift the barriers in OGD.

Action IV.   Align digital laws with the requirements of OGD.

Action V.   Create directives for government institutions regarding the legal restrictions and new legislations about government data.

Step 5. Promote Public Data Release Widely and Assign Responsibilities

Opening up government data is a multi layered procedure and involves contributions from all levels of government, from government ministries all the way to government agency employees. It's important that government departments identify specific assignments for each role as well as the responsibilities that follow that role, so that the information being provided is handled as an asset and delicately. Special roles should be designed to manage data openness in the institutional and governmental level. In the government level and institutional level for each department there should be officers that explain how open data holds a strategic advantage to both the public and the stakeholders. This is especially important in the initial phases when the outcomes of OGD are yet to be realized.

There should be responsible departments to ensure data quality and openness when OGD policies are being implemented. This role should check the issues regarding the datasets released such as: data formats, usability, accessibility, legal and regulatory breaches, positive and negative feedbacks from users etc.

In order to promote innovation of new applications and services out of OGD initiatives there should be departments to facilitate the use of public use of data by developers and businesses as well as government agencies. In case there is a need for guidance or consultation about practical issues regarding the datasets, these departments should communicate the requirements to the entrepreneurs. Data safety and confidentiality issues should be addressed by this authority as well.

In order to ensure interoperability and cooperation between government agencies -especially among those that use similar data and formats- there should be a cooperative management body to settle the communication between the stakeholders.

Set of Actions

Action I.   Design special roles to manage data openness in the institutional and governmental level and assign responsible officers to manage OGD initiatives.

Action II.   Design special roles and assign officers that will communicate the strategic advantages and benefits of OGD in the institutional and governmental level

Action III.   Set responsible departments to ensure data quality and openness when OGD policies are being implemented

Action IV.   Assign roles to certain departments to facilitate the public use of data by developers and businesses as well as government agencies.

Action V.   Set up a cooperative management body to settle the communication between the stakeholders in order to ensure interoperability and cooperation between government agencies.

Step 6. Choose Suitable Data Format for Common Usability

Datasets should be usable and accessible by everyone. Therefore, depending on the requirements of the nature of the data in hand, most common and usable formats should be chosen when opening the government data. In general, there are a variety of different formats to choose from. One of the most well known format, is HTML. In order for the data to be used efficiently, it must be provided in a format that is usable on a range of different platforms, which means that format must be an "open format". Open formats allow data to be opened on programs other than the program that it was originally created in, making it the best choice. XML, CSV and RDF are also commonly used and widely accepted formats that can prove the most suitable for a wide range of datasets.

Patent restrictions should not apply on the reuse of the data which is under the public sector, and therefore the data must be given on standard computer formats in order to optimize its use and reuse.

It is also important to publish data in different formats for different users. By publishing new or updated data in a variety of different formats, the whole process of accessing and viewing data becomes easier and a wider range of users would be covered.

Set of Actions

Action I.	Analyze the public datasets and choose appropriate formats for these to publish.
Action II.	Analyze which formats are commonly used widely accepted.
Action III.	Choose open formats to publish public data.
Action IV.	Instruct government departments on the accessibility, usability and interoperability issues regarding the data formats used.
Action V.	Publish data in different formats for different user requirements.

Step 7. Establish a Central Storage and Access Point for All Government Data

Each government holds a huge amount of data in different classifications and by different departments. In order for users to access the data conveniently, setting up a central data portal makes it easier to facilitate publishing data from a central access point. Users would be able to look for relevant datasets, make filtered searches, access the documentation and data usage statistics through the portal. Linking related data and creating taxonomies for different departments and different datasets would increase findability of the published data.

Governments should also keep track of their data assets continuously from the very early development stages of the open data policy. This allows not only the government, but also the stakeholders too, to be entirely aware of the potential that open data holds. Governments should take the time to review any existing data, including data that would be beneficial if it were to be structured data, even though definition data is a difficult task to take on.

Set of Actions

Action I.   Set up a central point of access for all the published government data.

Action II.   Include guidelines to use published data in the data portal, clearly state restrictions and usage rights.

Action III.   Provide that every government institution publish their datasets in the central platform or link their data to the portal.

Action IV.   Include resources about the overall open data strategy, guidelines to open institutional data, and instructions about legal laws and regulations regarding OGD.

Action V.   Link datasets to each other to increase find-ability of the required data.

Action VI.   Create taxonomies and classifications of the published data and document data properties of each dataset.

Step 8. Publish the Data

Publishing government data is a never ending process. Governments hold bulks of historical data and keep collecting data from various sources by different means. We have discussed that governments hold statistical data, sensor based data as well as user generated data on a continuous basis. Therefore, open government data requires a constant effort to release timely data at all times.

For the start, the most efficient, fastest, and simplest way to publish government data, is publishing the available datasets online in its raw and original state. While its raw state is important, structuring it properly is equally as important, and this allows the data to be used within an automated system. Publishing data which can only be seen rather than extracted is not as useful, therefore should be avoided as much as possible.

Governments and government agencies should carry on a well designed workflow to keep publishing the datasets abiding with the principles of OGD that we already have discussed, namely: complete, primary, timely, accessible, machine-readable, nondiscriminatory, nonproprietary and license-free.

Each government entity should be directed to publish their datasets in the central government data portal starting from the available and prioritized datasets and encouraged to improve the quality and quantity of the data they release. Formatting issues, security and privacy concerns, usability and accessibility issues should all be addressed by the central and local government agencies.

Set of Actions

Action I. Publish the data in its raw state abiding with the principles of OGD.

Action II. Set up a strict workflow that ensures constantly publishing available datasets for all government departments.

Action III. Direct the government agencies to prioritize, publish, and improve the datasets and guide them to stick to the standards for usability, security and accessibility issues.

Step 9. Make Data Useful

Published data requires some additional properties so that it is not only existent but also useful for varying purposes. We have already discussed the formatting issues, accessibility and the importance of data standardization. From the innovation perspective, if governments pursue creation of new services and applications through OGD, up-to-date real time information proves vital.

Publishing data through an Application Programming Interface (API) which have become increasingly popular over the recent years is a key enabler to deploy new services through public and private initiatives. APIs allow programmers and developers the ease of accessing certain parts of data rather than in bulk. The biggest benefit to using an API is that it is connected to a database and therefore updates in real time, which makes the data available the most recent data. In the examples from the UK, USA and Singapore several government departments make their data available through APIs, which give service developers a great deal of flexibility on the reuse of the data for the purposes of the services being created utilizing open public data. Software developers may use the same APIs and tweak them depending on the nature of service so that they are able to create different applications using the same datasets. Singapore's Land Transport Authority provides open data through APIs and there have been several public transportation apps, live traffic update services as well as driving route planner apps created by making use of these APIs provided.

Making use of metadata also improves the data usability. Metadata simply provides a description of the data which the user is about to access which is useful to the user, providing them with the chance to decide whether or not that is the data that they are looking for, and move on to the next piece of data if it is not. Metadata plays a key part in making your data more discoverable on the internet. Strong metadata schemes enable data publishers to classify certain aspects of their datasets, and this classification allows the data to be discovered easier.

Set of Actions

Action I.   Instruct government organizations about how open data may lead to create new services and applications.

Action II.   Encourage government agencies to provide APIs with their datasets.

Action III.   Increase data discoverability by mandating metadata usage in published data.

4.1. Implications for MobileGovernment

Governments should also work on realizing the potential of OGD in mobileGovernment development. This is an integral part of "making data useful" as discussed in Step 9 in the previous section. Government policies on OGD should include guidance on how to make published datasets useful for mobile platforms. APIs prove useful for developers to create mobile applications, therefore government entities should be encouraged to deliver APIs with the released data wherever it is feasible.

Private initiatives should be mobilised to work in partnership with citizens and governments in order to develop useful services for public. OGD, in principle, provides great opportunities to bring together end users, service developers and government departments, and give way to design-enabled innovation where the focus is the end-users' experience that employ bottom-up initiatives rather than providing top-down public services and applications.

Next section will contain more detail on the use of OGD in mobileGovernment projects.

5. Government Open Data Going Mobile: Opportunities & Challenges for mobileGovernment Development

Governments, as discussed, are opening vast amount of data sets for public use and redistribution in new innovative ways. As the quality and amount of data released increase, more sophisticated use of this data to create services and applications increase too. Thus, open government data presents itself as an inevitably relevant aspect of mobileGovernment developments globally. Moreover, the growing amount and quality of government data is a big treasure for the potential developments in the field of mobileGovernment.

Opportunities arising from government data openness is not only limited to the fact that OGD presents new possibilities of service creation and delivery, but also, that it enables participation of all stakeholders (citizens, businesses and government departments) in developing new public services by engaging users in data collection and sharing.

5.1. Opportunities for MobileGovernment

In this section, two key dimensions of open government data will be discussed that present themselves as unique opportunities for mobileGovernment development. First section discusses how opening government data may contribute to innovation in public services and the second section argues that OGD does also catalyze private initiatives from businesses and individuals to take part in mobile service creation either by reusing published data or acting as a data source for services that exploit user-generated data.

5.1.1. Innovative Mobile Services Using Open Government Data

OGD has the potential to enable several mobile services by allowing users to:

- Access relevant public information on the go
- Observe government performance in service delivery
- Contribute to open discussions about public matters and give opinion "on the spot"
- Report issues and share public problems with other interested parties (filing complaints, report problems and offences etc.)
- Access real time data from centrally managed databases (traffic, weather, events etc.)
- Contribute as a data provider and take part in mobile service creation (share GPS data for traffic apps, report road incidents or public issues locally etc.)

There are hundreds of examples of mobile service applications created either by government agencies or private initiatives by utilizing the published government datasets around the world. Some governments even showcase mobile application catalogues that are facilitated by opening up government data. In the US, www.data.gov/applications website lists OGD applications most of which are also in mobile platform. Canada presents its Open Data apps in its official app store - http://open.canada.ca/en/apps. European union lists its open government applications in this list: https://open-data.europa.eu/en/apps.

In the US OGD, for instance, the published datasets are accompanied by useful tools to make the published datasets useful. Datasets are searchable and easy to find with detailed descriptions of its content. Several categories of datasets are supported by metadata so that humans as well as machines can extract the data on request.

The developed mobile and web applications that utilize these data are also listed categorically. Moreover, for application developers, there are several tools and guiding documents to help them develop useful application with the datasets. APIs (Application Programming Interface) are also provided with the datasets in many of the cases, and these are free to use commercially and for private purposes without restriction.

Public data as discussed is generally in a raw form. Applications created are visual representations of these data in a purposeful way. It is found that the resource data for these mobile applications are generally statistical data, sensor based data or user generated data. Public agencies hold statistics about the population, crime, accidents, health issues, economic indicators and all sorts of statistical data. There are also sensor based data that generally local governments hold such as traffic volume, parking space availability, weather temperature, traffic light information, river flows etc. Lastly, in some cases there are types of data that are gathered from users. Examples are mobile phone signal utilization to estimate traffic volume and speed, GPS based data gathered from users, complaint and feedback applications about various subjects such as restaurants, public issues and help exchange apps. Mainka's analysis of local government mobile applications finds that there are variety of services ranging from informational services, mobility and tourism applications to education, health and public safety, utilizing the datasets that governments open.

Mobile applications that utilize OGD are visualized and organized forms of the datasets. For instance, the "Dublin Parking" application provides disabled parking availability in the Dublin city, and users can plan their journeys depending on the availability of the parking space using this mapping application. Mapping functionality is very common in the OGD mobile applications, such as nearest hospital and pharmacy applications ("UK Pharmacy"), traffic applications and local public transport applications. Another example that mapping functionality is used is the "USA Jobs" application that provides users an interface to search for job vacancies in their proximity and even apply for these jobs. "Crime in Chicago" application allows users to find out facts about the criminal cases and statistics about their neighborhood and other parts of the city. Also in Singapore, we see several advanced form of OGD applications that provide services with mapping functionality such as real time traffic data, shortest/fastest driving route, public transport planner, points of interest and tourist guide apps. As it is evident from these cases, the possibilities are endless when the datasets are released in reusable formats.

5.1.2. Involving Users in Mobile Service Development through OGD

The role of governments in public service delivery is shifting from being the service developer and provider towards being the key enabler of service creation and development by private initiatives especially in ICT related services and applications. Governments evidently can not always catch up with the fast pace of changes in technology usage among the citizens, therefore they should involve the users (citizens, private businesses) in public service innovation or in many cases, create an environment that private initiatives can contribute with their own ideas and resources.

Opening government data publicly sparks social innovation by engaging users and developers in service development as well as opening up ways to create services utilizing user-generated data. This dramatically shifts the idea that citizens are merely consumers of public services, and leads us to user-driven innovation and co-creation concepts.

User-driven innovation methodology is based on the idea that users (consumers, citizens, businesses, government employees etc) should be central actors in service design and development, moreover they should be actively engaged in all stages from idea generation to the final implementation. This is especially the case for mobileGovernment services and applications.

When public datasets are available in reusable formats, individual users, businesses and developers can take part in designing useful applications and services by transforming raw datasets into purposeful services and applications for public use. As a result, public sector offloads some of the responsibility to create services using available datasets over to private initiatives. Moreover, end users can also participate in mobileGovernment services by sharing own data.

There has been a lot of successful examples of crowd-sourced mobile services especially where real-time data is crucial for the service provided. In many large cities, such as Barcelona, Singapore, Vienna, Hong Kong and Amsterdam, there are growing amount of initiatives to build mobile applications utilizing government datasets that are made public. Initiatives are generally overtaken by partnerships between individuals, businesses, NGOs, universities, and local public authorities.

Some of the leading examples in the world are Singapore, Hong Kong and Bahrain who has many innovative mobile applications that are based on OGD. These applications were developed not only with government initiative but also by individuals and private sector developers who all are using the datasets opened by the governments in these countries. There are simple informational applications as well as more sophisticated services among them and they may be considered as prime examples of how opening government data leads to innovations. OGD is basically the enabler of these applications and services.

Mobilising public private initiatives towards reusing government held data in order to create new services is rather new but hugely promising phenomena in mobileGovernment's evolving nature. By extensive use and reuse of government open data, innovative mobile public services will flourish with bottom-up and top-down initiatives employing relevant partnerships between private and public sector.

5.2. Some Challenges of Open Government Data for mobileGovernment

Opening government data is a wholesome project that requires alignment of several factors within the public sector. These present the planning authorities with huge challenges. Most importantly, the task in hand is not just publishing the datasets but also fostering innovation and efficiency in result. Thus, this section will discuss the challenges ahead of OGD in two respects: first, the challenges to open government data in general, and second, challenges to efficiently utilize public data specifically for mobileGovernment services development.

5.2.1. General Challenges to Open Government Data

- **Strategic Planning:** OGD requires general planning and wholesome strategy carefully designed taking into account the unique targets and obstacles for governments. Although many countries have OGD in their agenda to achieve their OGD targets, many times public decision making processes struggling for the pace required to form a central strategy and move ahead to achieve targets.

- Lack of a dedicated government strategy presents an obstacle for other challenges of OGD that will be discussed below, such as planning, budget, legislation, and organisational transformation.

- **Organisational Frictions:** Governments, like any other institution, work within a set of culture that is formed over time. It is a daunting task to adjust organisational culture towards a more transparent and publicly open setting. OGD brings a lot of advantages to government entities, however, it is still a big effort to open all the required datasets, therefore, there will be a certain level of resistance to make government departments to publish their datasets due to technical, economical, organisational or legal issues. This is why strong leadership, detailed strategy and right incentives need to be set to achieve OGD targets.

- **Technical Obstacles:** Different technical requirements will emerge as government departments start to publish their datasets. Thus, governments and its departments should be aware of the technological requirements of their projects and invest in ICT as well as employee skill's development. New softwares, technological equipments and varying connectivity issues are going to pose obstacles for OGD.

- **Cooperation Between Government Departments:** Many leading examples of OGD initiatives such as Singapore and United States employ a central portal for government datasets where different departments can publish their data. Some of these datasets require efficient communication and cooperation between government departments in order to solve security and data quality issues as well as to avoid duplications. Therefore government departments need to work closely together to be in line with the overall targets and strategy.

- **Providing Data Continuously and in Good Quality:** Published government data should be delivered to meet initially set standards and quality in order to be useful. Because the main aim of publishing government data is to make it reusable for interested parties. Therefore, government entities have the challenge to adapt their available datasets to the standards and continuously publish up-to-date data abiding the principles set initially. Opening government data is a continuous process that requires periodical or real-time updates from all departments.

- **Security and Privacy:** Public offices hold sensitive and confidential data, and opening up public information is a risky business. The first and foremost concern when releasing public data, therefore, has to be to keep sensitive information safe and disclosed. This requires technical and organisational awareness about the possible dangers of publishing public data and needs to be addressed properly by central and local government departments.

- **Legal Challenges:** Opening government data may have complications in legal aspects and there may be a need to pass new regulations and legislations in order to overcome legal restrictions. New regulations should pay attention to ownership and usage rights, privacy and confidentiality issues, and possible misuse cases for government data.

5.2.2. Challenges for MobileGovernment Service Developments

Utilizing government datasets to design mobile services and applications also poses its own challenges apart from the aforementioned challenges of open government data.

- **Promoting Open Data Use:** Opening government data leads to government transparency straight away in principle, however, it does not automatically lead to a more efficient government. Opened up data should be used and reused in as many useful ways as possible in order to have an added value. Getting public sector departments, businesses and citizens to make use of the OGD is entirely a different challenge than releasing government datasets.

- Governments should lead the way to showcase the opportunities that OGD presents by extensively utilizing the datasets in public services. Therefore, promotion of OGD should start targeting the government departments initially and encouraging them to utilize government held data in creating innovative services and applications.

- Government employees should be made aware of the infinite possibilities of delivering public services on mobile platforms by utilizing government data.

- **Security of Mobile Apps and Software:** Sensitive government data requires special treatment wherever it is being used. Mobile platforms may threaten government data security and public data confidentiality if applications and services are not designed to meet the security and privacy standards. Therefore special attention to mobile security of public data that takes device properties, software security issues and connection security into account needs to be developed prior to mobile service creation.

- **Usability and Design Issues on Mobile:** In order to create new mobile services and applications, released datasets should be usable in mobile platforms. Government entities should be incentivized to design APIs with their released datasets in order for other stakeholders to freely integrate those data in creating innovative applications. APIs enable programmers to attain relevant data from huge datasets with queries so designing applications that serve specific needs utilizing bulks of government datasets.

- **Encouraging Individual and Private Sector Initiatives:** The most promising aspect of opening government data is that it may lead to innovation in public services not only by the government initiative but also with the contribution of other stakeholders including businesses and citizens. Therefore, private sector stakeholders and creative individuals should also be mobilised to contribute in service creation. Successful promotion of OGD initiatives in mobile platform is a challenge that requires strong leadership and dedication from the government departments themselves and it should lead to a productive environment that innovative mobile services flourish with the efforts of private initiatives and citizens.

- **Forming Mutually Beneficial Private-Public Partnerships:** Governments should seek to form partnerships with stakeholders across the mobile value chain that will enable new public services that utilize government data. There are vast amount of specialists and entrepreneurs in the mobile value chain and getting them to collaborate in public service design together with government departments will lead to integrated advanced forms of mobile public services. For instance, mobile payment services that are designed in partnership with banks and government tax offices; municipal traffic applications using software of GPS device manufacturers; real time road condition tracking with sensors from IT companies collaborating with Road Transport authorities are good examples of public private partnerships utilizing OGD in mobile platforms.

6. Conclusion

Governments at the age of this "data revolution" are now beyond questioning whether they should open the government data or not. Open data is becoming the norm and the question that the governments are facing now is rather how to open government data to the best use in their country's own context. Governments should carefully study the potential in OGD and promote it for all the stakeholders starting from the government institutions themselves.

Government departments must realize that OGD will bring various advantages in internal government business processes including but not limited to: interoperability between systems and software, and applications that are used by different departments; enhanced communication between government entities and resulting efficiency gains in the workflow; increased transparency that will build trust and citizen engagement in public interactions; new opportunities to create new services and increase public service quality; huge reduction in public requests for information as well as time consuming operations within government's internal workflow and so on.

OGD is also undeniably a vital part of mobileGovernment. It does open up unprecedented opportunities for mobileGovernment development. New mobile services utilizing only government held data are already underway in many of the developing and developed countries. However, the full potential is yet to be realized. Therefore mobileGovernment strategies of governments should place special emphasis on the opportunities that emerge via OGD developments.

The OGD strategy should also be designed to attract businesses and citizens to fully engage and make use of the public data. Potential benefits of OGD should be communicated to all the stakeholders and a cumulative contribution should be encouraged to make the most out of OGD initiatives.

Bibliography:

- "App Showcase - data.gov.sg." 2015. 17 May. 2016 <https://ref.data.gov.sg/AppShowcase/AppList.aspx>
- Helbig, Natalie et al. "The dynamics of opening government data." *Center for Technology in Government.[Online]. Available: http://www. ctg. albany. edu/publications/reports/opendata* (2012).
- "Principles - Project Open Data." 2014. 17 May. 2016 <https://project-open-data.cio.gov/principles/>
- "How to Open up Data - The Open Data Handbook." 2015. 17 May. 2016 <http://opendatahandbook.org/guide/en/how-to-open-up-data/>
- Mainka, A. "Mobile Application Services Based Upon Open Urban ... - Ideals." 2015. <https://www.ideals.illinois.edu/bitstream/handle/2142/73635/114_ready.pdf?sequence=2>
- Janssen, Katleen. "Open government data and the right to information: Opportunities and obstacles." *The Journal of Community Informatics* 8.2 (2012).
- Chan, CML. "From Open Data to Open Innovation Strategies - IEEE Computer Society." 2013. <https://www.computer.org/csdl/proceedings/hicss/2013/4892/00/4892b890.pdf>
- "Service innovation: the hidden value of open data" 2015. 17 May. 2016 <https://www.w3.org/2013/share-psi/workshop/krems/papers/ServiceInnovation-theHiddenValueOfOpenData>
- "About Us - Data.gov.sg." 2015. 9 May. 2016 <https://data.gov.sg/about>
- "Singapore makes strides in Open Data | iN.SG." 2014. 9 May. 2016 <https://www.ida.gov.sg/blog/insg/special-reports/singapore-makes-strides-in-open-data/>
- "Key Findings - Open Data Barometer." 2016. 17 May. 2016 <http://opendatabarometer.org/2ndEdition/summary/>

- "A World That Counts - Data Revolution Group." 2014. 17 May. 2016 <http://www.undatarevolution.org/wp-content/uploads/2014/12/A-World-That-Counts2.pdf>
- "Open Data — Code for America." 2015. 17 May. 2016 <https://www.codeforamerica.org/practices/open/open-data/>
- "Open Data Policy Guidelines - Sunlight Foundation." 2013. 17 May. 2016 <http://sunlightfoundation.com/opendataguidelines/>
- "Project Open Data - CIO Council." 2014. 17 May. 2016 <https://project-open-data.cio.gov/>
- Chan, Calvin ML. "From open data to open innovation strategies: Creating e-services using open government data." *System Sciences (HICSS), 2013 46th Hawaii International Conference on* 7 Jan. 2013: 1890-1899.
- Loutas, Nikolaos, Anastasia Varitimou, and Vassilios Peristeras. "Unraveling the mystery of Open Government Data Apps." *WORKSHOP ON USING OPEN DATA: POLICY MODELING, CITIZEN EMPOWERMENT, DATA JOURNALISM* Feb. 2013.
- "Background and Introduction - Open Data Barometer." 2016. 17 May. 2016 <http://opendatabarometer.org/2ndEdition/summary/the_barometer.html>
- "Slash Data Catalog Requirements - Project Open Data." 2014. 17 May. 2016 <https://project-open-data.cio.gov/catalog/>
- "Mobility and government - Municipal Information Systems Association." 2016. 17 May. 2016 <https://www.misa-asim.ca/resource/collection/18E66D50-AE69-458D-904B-BB0BDF52829E/Dalhousie_University_-_Mobility_Report.pdf>
- "Implementation Guide - Project Open Data." 2014. 17 May. 2016 <https://project-open-data.cio.gov/implementation-guide/>
- Ubaldi, B. "Open Government Data - eSPap." 2015. <https://www.espap.pt/Documents/espap_lab/2015_04_Open_Government_Data.pdf>

- "Slash Data Catalog Requirements - Project Open Data." 2014. 17 May. 2016 <https://project-open-data.cio.gov/catalog/>
- "Government Open Data: Benefits, Strategies, and Use." 2014. 17 May. 2016 <https://depts.washington.edu/esreview/wordpress/wp-content/uploads/2014/07/2014-Government-Open-Data.pdf>
- "Publishing Open Government Data - W3C." 2015. 17 May. 2016 <https://www.w3.org/TR/gov-data/>
- "Case study International Benchmark: Open data and use of standards ..." 2014. 17 May. 2016 <https://www.forumstandaardisatie.nl/fileadmin/os/documenten/Internationale_benchmark_v1_03_final.pdf>
- "Ten Principles for Opening Up Government ... - Sunlight Foundation." 2012. 17 May. 2016 <https://sunlightfoundation.com/policy/documents/ten-open-data-principles/>
- "Guidelines on Open Government Data for Citizen Engagement." 2013. 17 May. 2016 <http://workspace.unpan.org/sites/Internet/Documents/Guidenlines%20on%20OGDCE%20May17%202013.pdf>
- "Open Data — Code for America." 2015. 17 May. 2016 <https://www.codeforamerica.org/practices/open/open-data/>

A Short Bio of Emre Simsek

Emre Simsek, during recent years has worked as an expert researcher in mobileGovernment projects at the mobileGov UK. He is an Economist by formation and holds a BS degree in Economics, Bosphorus University in Istanbul.

He started working in the mobileGovernment field, initially researching the economic and developmental impacts of mobile government projects, in 2008. Since 2009, he took part in several the projects, researches and conferences along with Ibrahim Kushchu and built his expertise in mobileGovernment as a consultant and researcher.

Some of the ICT projects Simsek took part in mobileGovernment field include: /strategies for developing and deploying mGovernment applications and services for a private IT company in Sweden', The RoadMap for the UAE to move from eGovernment to Smart Government and ' preparation of guidelines for mobile services development for public sector organisations'.

A Short Bio of I. Kushchu

Ibrahim Kushchu is the founder of the field of MobileGovernment – the use of mobile technologies in the public sector to offer services to citizens. His expertise also cover community informatics, enterprise mobility, management systems and artificial intelligence. Combining his management studies and his expertise in artificial intelligence, Prof. Kushchu has been working for business schools in the UK and in Japan, and teaching various information communication technology courses especially related to ICT, electronic business and mobile business.

Prof. Kushchu is an internationally recognized pioneering practitioner and researcher in developing the mobileGovernment field by bringing into the light the issues related to the use of mobile

technologies in electronic government. His work also extends to impact of mobile technologies on economic and social development. He has developed strategies and road map for mobileGovernment for various countries in the world including recent ones in Afghanistan and the United Arab Emirates.

In addition to working with governments, and he has been working with various multi-national organizations including GATES FOUNDATION, CISCO, NOKIA, HITACHI, and NTT DoCoMo at projects involving consultancy, research, and educational events. He also offers advisory services to local and central government organization and their agencies.

He has edited and co-edited three books and has a number of publications in various international journals and in the proceedings of reputable conferences. He is also very active in international community of researchers through speaking, organizing, chairing, co-chairing various international conferences, and serving in the committees.

Prof. Kushchu holds a first degree (BSc) in management. He also has an MBA and a Master's degree (MSc) in artificial intelligence from the University of Edinburgh, UK. He was awarded a PhD degree in evolutionary artificial intelligence from the University of Sussex

ABOUT mobileGov UK

mobileGov UK offers effective strategic consultancy services based on its influential activities in MobileGovernment(TM) practice and approaches and leads mGov(TM) services to citizens in the EU and in countries such as Japan, UAE, Korea, Canada, Afghanistan and Turkey.

- Our company has been influencing many governments' strategies for mobileGovernment.
- Our company is the founder and the world leader of mGovernment Practice.
- Our company is the only organization having a comprehensive knowledge of history and current developments of International mGovernment Practice.
- Our company created and works with the largest and effective network of government organizations, international experts and other relevant stakeholders:
- Our company holds the only existing international conference on mobileGovernment and relevant conferences on mobile development and society (pleas see **www.m4life.org**):
- Our company builds upon years of experience in the mGovernment practice.

In short, Our company offers quality mGovernment advisory services based on its comprehensive knowledge of the field and other governments' experiences, the network of key expertise and ability conduct international training programs and seminars. For more feel free to visit: www.mgovernment.net.

Trademarks and Licensing

mGov, mGovernment, mobileGov and mobileGovernment are trademarks of mobileGov UK. Unlicensed use is prohibited. Please write to ik@mgovernment.net or visit www.mgovernment.net for licensing or permission